ORIGAMI

sort-of-difficult
ORIGAMI

by Chris Alexander

Capstone
press®
Mankato, Minnesota

Snap Books are published by Capstone Press,
151 Good Counsel Drive, P.O. Box 669, Mankato, Minnesota 56002.
www.capstonepress.com

Library of Congress Cataloging-in-Publication Data
Alexander, Chris.
    Sort-of-difficult origami / by Chris Alexander.
    p. cm. — (Snap books. Origami)
    Includes bibliographical references and index.
    Summary: "Provides step-by-step instructions for moderately difficult origami models, including a fox mask,
a tulip and stem, a masu box and insert, a penguin, a seal, a goldfish, a waterbomb, and an ornament" — Provided
by publisher.
    ISBN-13: 978-1-4296-2023-9 (hardcover)   *4142 3772   10/09*
    ISBN-10: 1-4296-2023-4 (hardcover)
    1. Paper work — Juvenile literature. I. Title.
TT870.A366 2009
736'.982 — dc22   2007052208

Editor: Christopher L. Harbo
Designer: Bobbi Wyss
Photo Researcher: Dede Barton
Photo Stylist: Sarah L. Schuette
Scheduler: Marcy Morin

Photo Credits:

All principal photography in this book by Capstone Press/Karon Dubke
Capstone Press/TJ Thoraldson Digital Photography, steps (all)
William Edwards Photography, 32

1 2 3 4 5 6 13 12 11 10 09 08

TABLE OF CONTENTS

page 8

page 14

page 22

Introduction and Materials 4

How to Use this Book 6

FOX MASK 8

WATERBOMB 10

ORNAMENT 12

TULIP AND STEM 14

MASU BOX AND INSERT 17

FANCY GOLDFISH 20

SEAL 22

PENGUIN 25

Fun Facts 28

What's Next 29

Glossary 30

Read More 31

Internet Sites 31

About the Author 32

Index 32

INTRODUCTION

Have you ever made a paper airplane or a paper fortune-teller? Then you've done origami. Now it's time to step up your folding skills. The seal, penguin, tulip, and other models in this book are challenging. But the finished models will definitely amaze your friends and family.

To get started, all you'll need are square pieces of paper and a little patience. Remember, practice is the key to success. If your model doesn't turn out the way it should, don't worry. Crumple it up and tell your friends you've made a basketball. Then score two points in the recycle bin and try the model again. The more times you practice a model, the better it will look.

MATERIALS

Traditionally, origami uses a single square of paper. Cutting and taping pieces of paper are not allowed. You can buy origami paper in most craft stores, on the Internet, and in some bookstores. It's usually colored on one side and white on the other. However, using official origami paper isn't necessary. You can cut squares from copy paper, newspapers, magazines, wrapping paper, or even aluminum foil. For origami, you can use almost any type of material that will stay in place when folded.

HOW TO USE THIS BOOK

Origami models are made with valley folds and mountain folds.
All other folds are just combinations of these two basic folds.

Valley folds are represented by a dashed line. The paper is creased along the line as the top surface of the paper is folded against itself like a book.

Mountain folds are represented by a pink dashed and dotted line. The paper is creased along the line and folded behind.

Reverse folds are made by opening a pocket slightly and folding the model inside itself along existing creases.

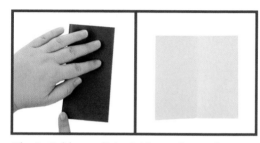

Mark folds are light folds used to make reference creases for a later step. Ideally, a mark fold will not be seen in the finished model.

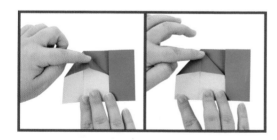

Squash folds are formed by lifting one edge of a pocket and reforming it so the spine gets flattened. The existing creases become new edges.

Outside reverse folds are two valley folds done at once. They are made by folding the model outside itself along existing creases.

Rabbit ear folds are formed by bringing two edges of a point together using existing creases. The new point is folded to one side.

FOLDING SYMBOLS

A crease from a previous step.	——————	Fold the paper in the direction of the arrow.	
A fold or edge hidden under another layer of paper; also used as an imaginary extension of an existing line.	· · · · · · · · · · · ·	Fold the paper and then unfold it.	
Turn the paper over or rotate it to a new position.		Fold the paper behind.	
Pleat the paper by reverse folding two creases.		Inflate the model by blowing air into it.	

FOX MASK

Traditional Model

Many origami models are flat and solid colored. The fox mask uses the white side of a colored piece of paper to highlight the ears. As an added bonus, the fox mask is an action model.

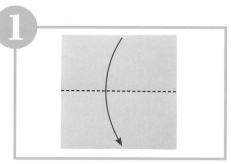

1

Start with the colored side down.
Valley fold in half.

2

Valley fold in half and unfold.

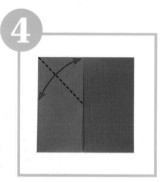

3

Valley fold both edges to the center.

4

Valley fold the top flap to the left edge and unfold.

5

Squash fold on the crease made in step 4.

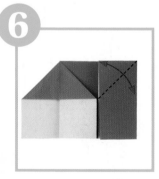

6

Repeat steps 4 and 5 on the right side.

7

Mountain fold the flaps to the back of the model.

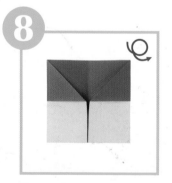

8

Rotate the paper.

9

Valley fold the top layer to the center.

10

Valley fold. The crease goes from corner to corner. The edge does not meet the center line.

11

Turn the paper over.

12

Repeat steps 9 and 10 on this side.

13

Valley fold the top flap to the right. Repeat behind.

14

Slowly spread the area marked A open while carefully pressing in at B.

15

Finished fox mask. Put your fingers inside the mask to open and close the mouth.

9

WATERBOMB

Traditional Model

The waterbomb model has been around for hundreds of years. Originally, it was filled with water and tossed like a water balloon. The model can also be used as a ball, an ornament, or dice.

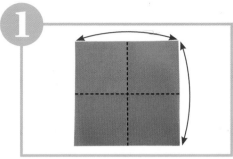

1

Start with the colored side up. Valley fold edge to edge in both directions and unfold.

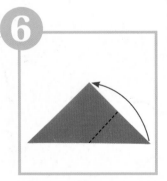

2

Turn the paper over.

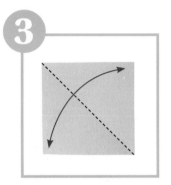

3

Valley fold point to point and unfold.

4

Valley fold point to point.

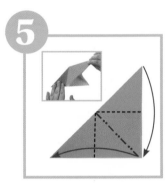

5

Squash fold.

6

Valley fold the top flap to the peak.

7

Mark fold the top flap in half and unfold.

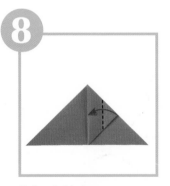

8

Valley fold the corner to the mark made in step 7.

9

Valley fold the top point to the corner made in step 8.

10

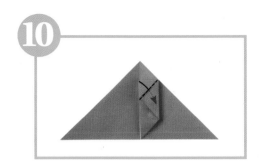

Valley fold the entire triangle into the pocket made in step 8.

11

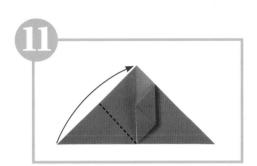

Repeat steps 6 through 10 on the left side.

12

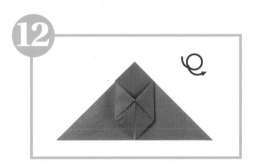

Turn the model over.

13

Repeat steps 6 through 11 on this side.

14

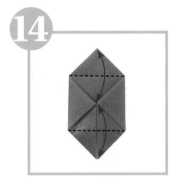

Valley fold to the center and unfold.

15

Gently blow into the hole at A to inflate the model.

16

Finished waterbomb.

11

ORNAMENT

Modular origami models, like this ornament, are made from several sheets of paper. As a rule, each sheet is folded into the same basic unit. Then the units are assembled together without using glue.

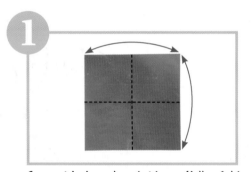

1 Start with the colored side up. Valley fold edge to edge in both directions and unfold.

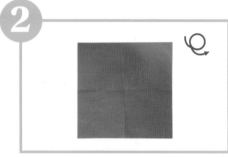

2 Turn the paper over.

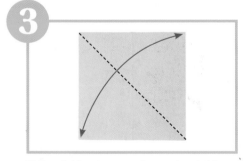

3 Valley fold point to point and unfold.

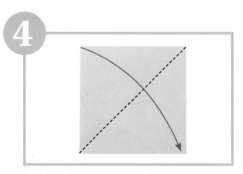

4 Valley fold point to point.

12

5

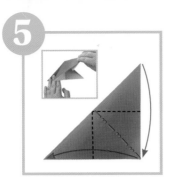

Squash fold.

6

Spread the points apart so it looks like an X from above.

7

Finished waterbomb unit. Repeat steps 1 through 6 to make five more units.

8

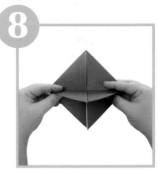

Place two units together so all four edges touch.

9

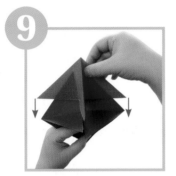

Place one unit over the top two points.

10

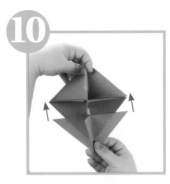

Place one unit over the bottom two points.

11

Place the next unit over points A and C.

12

Place point A into the pocket of point B.

13

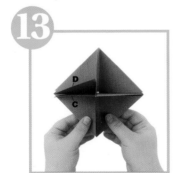

Place point C into the pocket of point D.

14

Repeat steps 11 through 13 with the last unit on the points in the back.

15

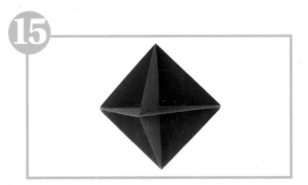

Finished ornament.

TULIP AND STEM

Traditional Model

Origami artists have invented many ways to fold tulips. This model is fun because it inflates like a balloon. Bring your tulip to life by mounting it on a stem.

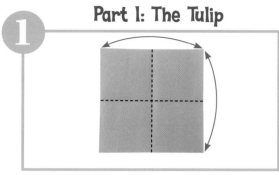

Part 1: The Tulip

1. Start with the colored side up. Valley fold edge to edge in both directions and unfold.

2. Turn the paper over.

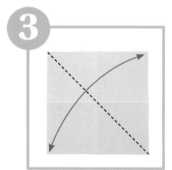

3. Valley fold point to point and unfold.

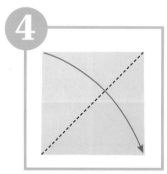

4. Valley fold point to point.

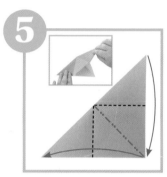

5. Squash fold.

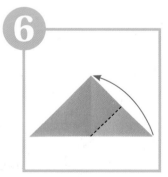

6. Valley fold the top flap to the peak.

7. Valley fold the top flap to the peak.

8. Turn the model over.

9. Repeat steps 6 and 7 on this side.

Valley fold the top flap from right to left.

Turn the model over.

Valley fold the top flap from right to left.

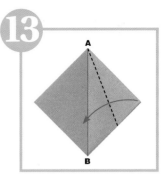

A

B

Valley fold the corner just past the center line AB.

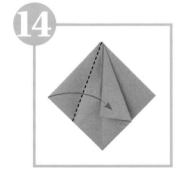

Repeat step 13 on the left side. Insert the corner of the top flap into the pocket.

Turn the model over.

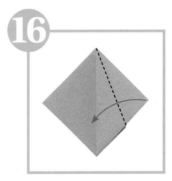

Repeat steps 13 and 14 on this side.

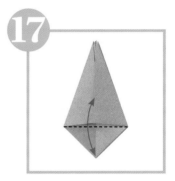

Valley fold and unfold.

18

Gently blow into the model at A forming a tall pyramid.

Part 2: The Stem

1

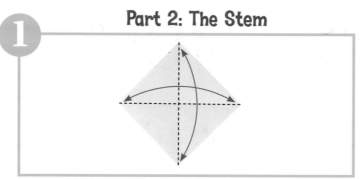

Start with the colored side down. Valley fold point to point in both directions and unfold.

2

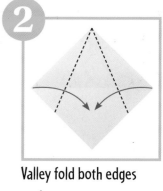

Valley fold both edges to the center.

19

Gently peel down the petals like you would peel a banana.

3

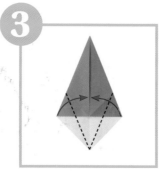

Valley fold both edges to the center.

4

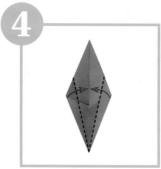

Valley fold both edges to the center.

5

Valley fold in half.

20

Finished tulip.

6

Valley fold in half.

7

Gently peel down the leaf like you would peel a banana.

8

Finished stem. Insert the stem into the blow hole of the tulip to display your flower.

MASU BOX AND INSERT

Traditional Model

Here is a simple project for storing your tiny keepsakes. Start with three pieces of paper, all the same size. One will be used for the insert, and the other two for the box and its lid.

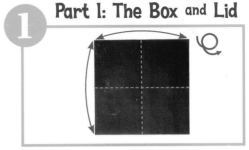

1 Start with the colored side up. Valley fold edge to edge in both directions and unfold. Then turn the paper over.

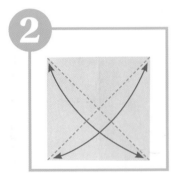

2 Valley fold point to point in both directions and unfold.

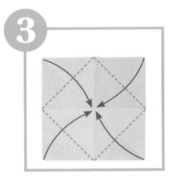

3 For a box, valley fold the corners to the center. For a lid, valley fold ⅛ of an inch from the center.

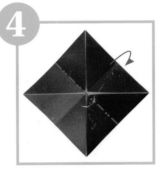

4 Mountain fold in half.

5 Valley fold the top layer in half. Repeat behind.

6 Unfold to step 4.

7 Repeat steps 4 through 6 on the opposite edges.

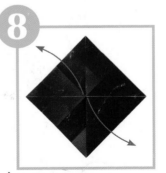

8 Unfold two opposite corners.

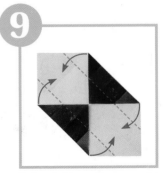

9 Valley fold to allow two sides of the box to stand up.

17

10 Fold up the third side of the box. The corners marked A will fold in against the inside of the box.

11 Valley fold the side in half and push the point into the center of the box.

12 Repeat steps 10 and 11 on the last side of the box.

13 Finished masu box.

Part 2: The Insert

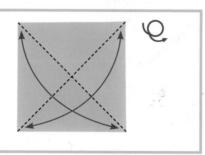

1 Start with the colored side up. Valley fold point to point in both directions and unfold. Then turn the paper over.

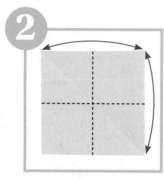

2 Valley fold edge to edge in both directions and unfold.

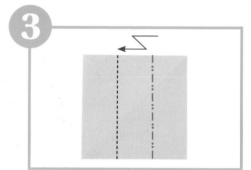

3 Gently pleat the paper into thirds. Adjust the paper until all three panels are equal, then crease sharply.

4 Unfold to step 3.

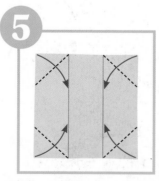

5 Valley fold the corners to the creases made in step 3.

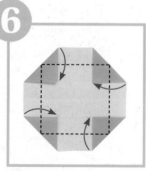

6 Valley fold the edges even with the corners.

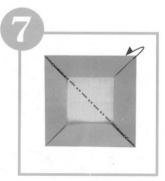

7 Mountain fold in half.

8

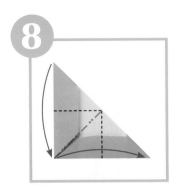

Squash fold on the creases made in steps 1 and 2.

9

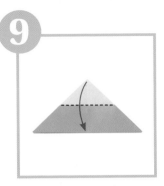

Valley fold the peak to the bottom edge.

10

Unfold the flap under the triangle. The model will be three dimensional.

11

Mountain fold in half. This joins the two As and the two Bs together.

12

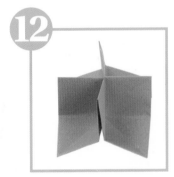

Reshape and reinforce all of the creases so the model will sit in the box.

13

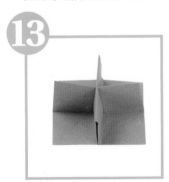

Finished insert. Place into the masu box.

FANCY GOLDFISH

Model designed by Chris Alexander

Some fancy goldfish can cost as much as $15,000. This model of a fancy goldfish will cost you only one square of paper. The finished model will be well worth the expense.

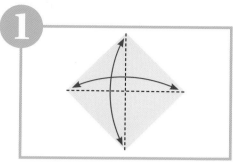

Start with the colored side down. Valley fold point to point in both directions and unfold.

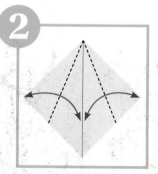

Valley fold the edges to the center and unfold.

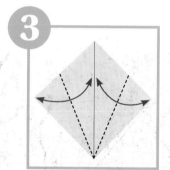

Valley fold the edges to the center and unfold.

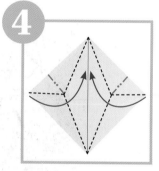

Rabbit ear fold using the creases made in steps 2 and 3.

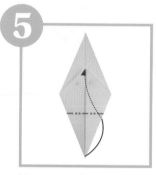

Mountain fold the bottom point. The point should be even with the tips of the flaps.

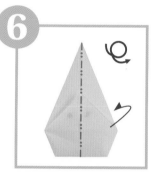

Mountain fold in half. Then rotate the model.

Valley fold and unfold. This crease starts about ⅓ of the way up the left edge.

Reverse fold on the crease made in step 7.

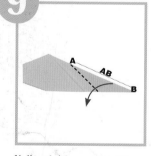

Valley fold so edge AB meets the tip of the flap.

Unfold to step 9.

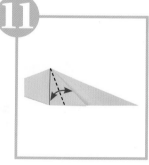

Valley fold the edge to the crease line and unfold. Repeat behind.

12

Squash fold to form the fin. Repeat behind.

13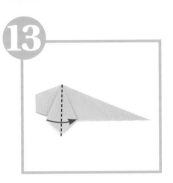

Valley fold the fin in half. Repeat behind.

14

Valley fold the top layer to the edge. Repeat behind.

15

Valley fold the flap back to the left. Repeat behind.

16

Outside reverse fold on the crease made in step 9.

17

Pull out the hidden paper inside the tail and place it on top of the tail. Repeat behind.

18

Valley fold the flap made in step 17 to the left. Repeat behind.

19

Finished fancy goldfish.

SEAL

Traditional Model

Seals can learn to perform all sorts of tricks. Likewise, this origami seal has a few tricks of its own to teach you. To complete the model, you'll need to perform several reverse folds.

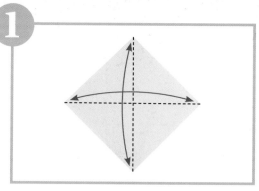

Start with the colored side down. Valley fold point to point in both directions and unfold.

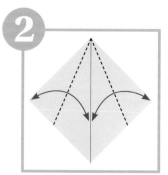

Valley fold both edges to the center and unfold.

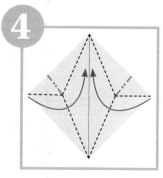

Valley fold both edges to the center and unfold.

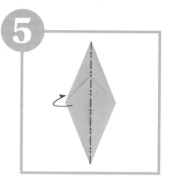

Rabbit ear fold using the creases made in steps 2 and 3.

Mountain fold in half.

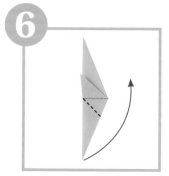

Valley fold the lower point to the right.

Unfold.

Reverse fold on the crease made in step 6.

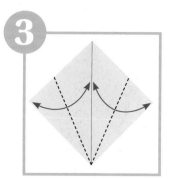

Rotate the model.

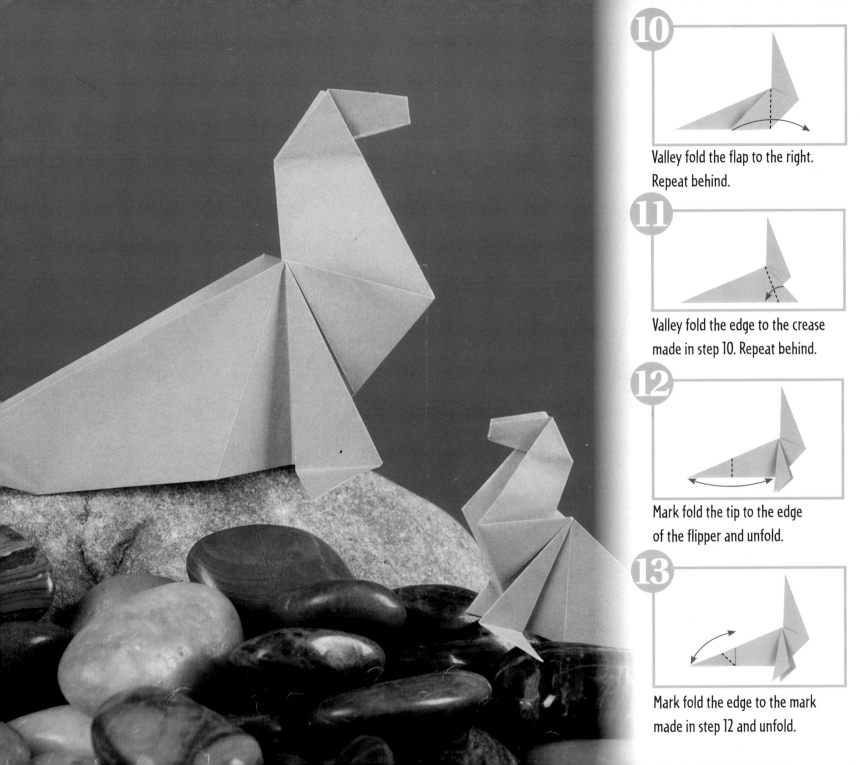

10 Valley fold the flap to the right. Repeat behind.

11 Valley fold the edge to the crease made in step 10. Repeat behind.

12 Mark fold the tip to the edge of the flipper and unfold.

13 Mark fold the edge to the mark made in step 12 and unfold.

23

Valley fold the edge to the mark made in step 13.

Unfold.

Reverse fold using the cease made in step 14.

Mark fold the point to about halfway between A and B.

Unfold to step 17.

Valley fold to the mark made in step 17 and unfold.

Reverse fold using the cease made in step 19.

Valley fold even with the chest and unfold.

Reverse fold using the cease made in step 21.

Valley fold the flippers outward so the model stands.

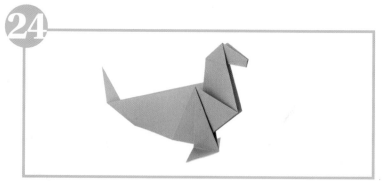

Finished seal.

PENGUIN

Traditional Model

Penguins are well adapted to life in the Antarctic. They can't fly, but their flipper-like wings make them strong swimmers. Folding the wings on this model will strengthen your origami skills. To form them, you'll practice a challenging rabbit ear fold.

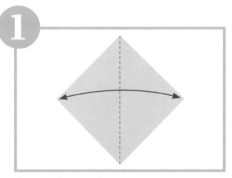

1

Start with the colored side down.
Valley fold point to point and unfold.

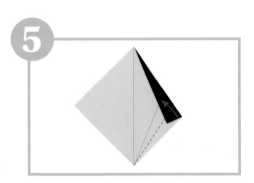

2

Valley fold to the center and unfold.

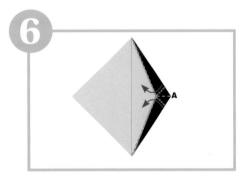

3

Valley fold to the center and unfold.

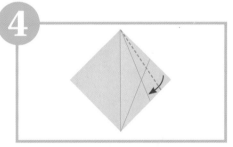

4

Valley fold to the crease made in step 2.

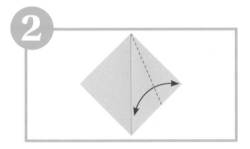

5

Valley fold to the crease made in step 3.

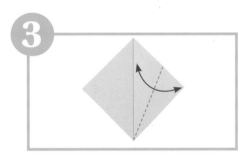

6

Rabbit ear fold using the creases made in steps 2 and 3. Carefully pinch the paper together at point A and lay it flat.

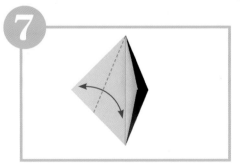

7

Repeat steps 2 through 6 on the left side.

25

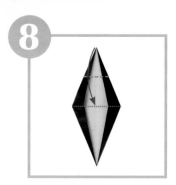

8

Valley fold the point to the center of the model.

9

Mark fold the point even with the tips of the wings and unfold.

10

Mountain fold the model in half.

11

Rotate the figure so edge AB is straight up and down.

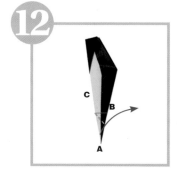

12

Valley fold. Edge AB forms a right angle with edge AC. The crease starts at the mark made in step 9.

13

Valley fold even with edge B.

14

Unfold to step 12.

15

Reverse fold on the crease made in step 12.

16

Reverse fold on the crease made in step 13.

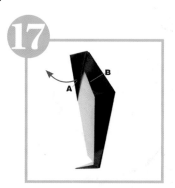

17

Pinch the model at B while pivoting A out to the left.

18

Valley fold the tip of the beak to the back of the head and unfold.

19

Valley fold the tip of the beak to the white corner and unfold.

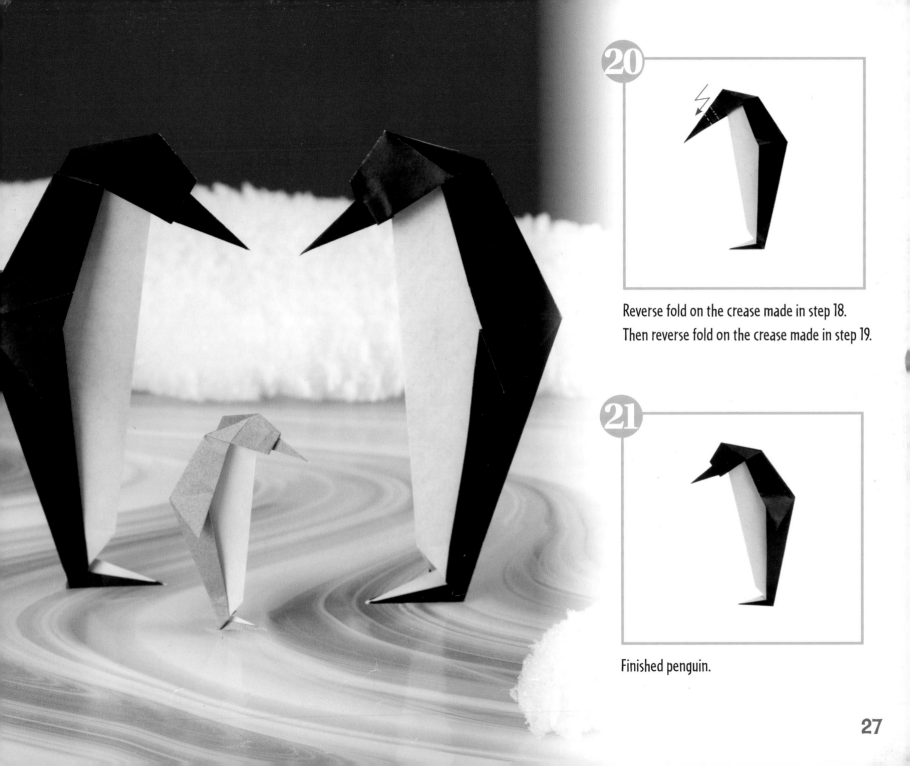

20

Reverse fold on the crease made in step 18.
Then reverse fold on the crease made in step 19.

21

Finished penguin.

FUN FACTS

In 2001, the largest paper crane was folded in the Odate Jukai Dome in Maebashi, Japan. It had a wingspan of 256 feet (78 meters).

The Red Sea Urchin, designed by Hans Birkeland, uses the most folds for a single model. The paper must be folded 913 times to create the model.

In 1967, the British Origami Society in London became the first organized origami society. OrigamiUSA formed in the United States in 1980.

The largest number of units used in a modular origami model is 2,200 units. These units form a wall mosaic showing the swan logo of the Origami Society Netherlands.

OrigamiUSA holds a convention each summer in New York City. The convention attracts origami masters and fans from all over the world. The convention gives people a chance see amazing origami models and learn more about the art.

Some people fold origami to express other hobbies and interests in their lives. Chris Alexander, the author of this book, creates models of the characters and spaceships from the *Star Wars* movies. Follow his link on FactHound (page 31) to see some of his amazing creations.

WHAT'S NEXT. . .

Now that you've mastered the models in this book, it's time to move on to more challenging projects. The next book in this series is *Difficult Origami*. In it you'll learn how to make a lop-eared rabbit, a speedboat, a picture frame, and many other models.

In addition to *Difficult Origami*, visit your local library and check out books by other artists. You will be amazed by what you can create with a simple piece of paper and a little imagination. Who knows, with enough practice you may become an origami master.

GLOSSARY

assemble (uh-SEM-buhl) — to put all the parts of something together

crease (KREESE) — to make lines or folds in something

fortune-teller (FOR-chuhn-TEL-ur) — someone or something that predicts the future

keepsake (KEEP-sayk) — something kept because it is special or valuable

modular (MOJ-ool-ur) — made up of several separate pieces or sections

mount (MOUNT) — to set in place for display

ornament (OR-nuh-muhnt) — a small, attractive object used for decoration

reverse (ri-VURSS) — opposite in position, order, or direction

READ MORE

Alexander, Chris. *Difficult Origami.* Origami. Mankato, Minn.: Capstone Press, 2009.

Montroll, John. *Birds and Insects Origami.* Mineola, N.Y.: Dover, 2004.

Sawyer, Brian, ed. *Napkin Origami: 25 Creative and Fun Ideas for Napkin Folding.* New York: Sterling, 2008.

INTERNET SITES

FactHound offers a safe, fun way to find Internet sites related to this book. All of the sites on FactHound have been researched by our staff.

Here's how:

1. Visit *www.facthound.com*
2. Choose your grade level.
3. Type in this book ID **1429620234** for age-appropriate sites. You may also browse subjects by clicking on letters, or by clicking on pictures and words.
4. Click on the **Fetch It** button.

FactHound will fetch the best sites for you!

ABOUT THE AUTHOR

Chris Alexander was born and raised in New York City. At the age of 5, he had his first experience with origami. During a visit to the public library, he came across a book with simple folding instructions. After successfully completing a paper cup, he was instantly hooked on the art. He insisted upon using the flimsy cup at dinner, but his mother urged him to learn other models instead. Almost 40 years and a multitude of "other models" later, Chris has created approximately 100 original models. Directions for one of them is found in this book.

INDEX

British Origami
Society, 28

common folds, 6–7

Fancy Goldfish,
20–21
folding symbols, 7
Fox Mask, 8–9

Masu Box and Insert,
17–19
materials, 5
modular origami,
12, 28

Origami Society
Netherlands, 28
OrigamiUSA, 28
Ornament, 12–13

paper cranes, 28
Penguin, 25–27

Seal, 22–24

Tulip and Stem,
14–16

Waterbomb, 10–11